Credit Repair Secrets

A Beginner's Guide to Fixing Credit, Managing Debt, and Raising Your Score

Julian Ashford

ISBN: 9781807650414

Published by TPSA Publishing

Table of Contents

INTRODUCTION

Most of us know that a poor credit score can prevent us from getting a loan or a credit card, but many of us don't know that it can also affect other areas of our lives, such as a poor credit score can prevent you from getting a job or a promotion. Employers are permitted by federal and many state laws to use their credit history in hiring decisions, believing that how someone handles their financial responsibilities is an indication of how well they might handle their work responsibilities as well.

Many people become enthusiastic about credit repairing, and when they see the effort involved and the time required on the journey to good credit, they get discouraged and give up. Others give up after the first negative response from a creditor or credit report agency, and some even go through with it but stop doing things to improve their credit when they've finished the process and still haven't managed to fix all the negative items. The important thing about the whole process is to stay motivated and continue improving. It will be extremely important throughout your life so that you can have fun and do the things you enjoy.

How much your credit status affects insurance is somewhat dependent on state laws. Your credit status may affect your rates or types of the homeowner, rental, or car insurance. Some auto insurance companies believe that poor credit correlates to higher accident risk and requires higher premiums.

Buying a home is a big step, and unless you can pay for it in cash, you will need a loan. This means everything involved comes down to your credit score and credit report. They will determine if you can even get a loan. If you can get a loan, they will determine the amount, type, and interest rate of the loan. It may also affect purchases you never thought about, such as your homeowner's insurance and necessities for the home, such as buying a refrigerator or a bed on credit.

The better your personal credit status is, the better chance you have of getting a start-up loan or a loan to expand your business. Most investors and lenders want to be confident in the financial status of the principals in the company, in particular their credit status. The theory being that if you cannot manage your own finances, how can you handle those of a business? Also, if you are selling a product and your credit status is good, the manufacturer of the product may be more likely to front you the product and allow you to pay for it after.

In fact, poor credit can easily cost you thousands of dollars a year in higher interest, larger fees, bigger premiums, extra loan points, and other hidden costs. Not only that, but a single negative item on your credit report will haunt you for years. On the other hand, having a high score will get you to credit when and where you need it. It increases your chances of landing better jobs, getting lower interest rates and fees. This is not only convenient but can save you thousands of dollars over some time.

Moreover, a poor credit score can keep you from renewing a professional license or prevent you from getting utilities or cable connections in your new apartment/home. It can also prevent you from posting bail for yourself or someone else. There are literally hundreds of ways a poor credit score can negatively impact your life, and what is more, it can do so for years to come if you do not act on it.

CHAPTER 1:
BASICS OF CREDIT REPAIR

It is hard to navigate today's society using credit. A variety of companies use your credit to choose how to place the pricing for services and goods that you use and also whether to do business. Consumers using a credit history seek out credit repair to increase their credit to have a simpler time.

What Is Bad Credit?

Bad credit is when you have missed one or more payments throughout your life, be it your fault or not. The most common mistake people make is not defaulting on a payment; it is actually delaying payments. It is usually when you forget about a deadline or can't find a certain bill, and you end up not paying, or being late, which in the eyes of the people borrowing money makes you look a bit financially unstable. Sometimes, even if you have had impeccable behavior, you are unfortunately affected by the loss of a job. Becoming unemployed has such grave consequences and leads to your assets being repossessed or even bankruptcy. Even if you went through a similar phase and you have bounced back, having this kind of history will negatively impact your credit report for a very long time.

It can also happen to you to be the victim of an error, even if you have not missed a single payment on your credit card until now. An error in the bank's system or an error from the parties responsible for building your credit report will affect you nonetheless, and so will fraud and abuse. Fraud cases are rare, but their consequences are costly. Fraud happens when someone uses your identity to submit a credit application, they get it, and then they do not repay it anymore. You will be contacted by the bank, and until you can prove you have been the target of a scam, you can have a tough time. Abuse generally refers to when you are oblivious to your expenses and spend over your credit card limit. You can wake up one day to a huge amount of debt, and cases of financial abuse most often end in you being forced to declare bankruptcy. To avoid these cases, you need to be very careful with your finances, but regardless of what your situation is, usually, there is a solution or a set of measures you can enforce to prevent it.

How to Avoid Bad Credit?

First of all, if you have lost your main source of income and are not able to make your payments in time or at all, you must say so. Announcing the fact that you may be unable to pay in the following months might land you a grace period from the lender. That means that you will not suffer any penalties for a given time until you can get back on your feet, maybe get a new job, and you can resume your normal payments.

You have to prioritize bills, meaning you will have to make a few judgment calls on what bills you should pay with the money you have left and which ones might be less likely to affect your credit. Keeping up with your bills is difficult, but it is also important if you do not want to end up with bad credit. Use your savings or whatever else you have available, and you may be able to make your credit look good even if you went through losing your job. These methods work to prevent credit, but they also apply in the case of you doing damage control. A credit repair will be a lot easier if you benefit from a grace period and do not have as many past due bills. It shows you were concerned and aware of the situation and that you tried your best to remain in control of your finances.

What Is Credit Repair?

Credit repair is the process in which credit standing is fixed, which might have declined due to various reasons. Credit standing might be as straightforward as disputing the information.

Another kind of credit fix is to take care of financial problems such as budgeting and start to deal with concerns.

How Credit Repair Works

Though companies claim they can clean up poor credit reports, correcting requires time and energy. A third party cannot remove the information. The specifics, incorrect or misrepresented, can be contested. Individuals are eligible for free credit reports every 12 months in addition to if an action is taken against them. Disputes may be registered if incorrect or incomplete information appears in their credit reports. Besides correcting such advice or grabbing fraudulent trades on one's credit, fixing and rebuilding credit may break more heavily on credit use and credit action. The payment history of this person may be a factor in their own credit standing. Taking measures to make certain payments are current or enhance the payment program for outstanding credit may negatively impact their credit rating. The total amount of credit may play a role. As an example, if somebody is actively using huge parts of the credit available to them, even if they are keeping minimum payments in time, how big the debt they are taking could negatively affect their credit score. The matter is their liquidity might be driven by the debt. They could see improvements by taking steps to decrease their debt burden.

CHAPTER 2: STEPS TO REPAIR YOUR CREDIT

Step 1. Get Your Credit Report

This step is crucial; banks and similar credit bureaus, which in turn hold the key to repairing the credit, report all credit information. Most people never consider getting their credit reports until they are trying to repair the credit, but it's always a good idea.

In most cases, there should be no charge for receiving a copy of your credit report; you simply have to request it (usually in writing, in person, and accompanied by a copy of your identification). When you are considered a bad creditor for a credit card or loan, the company must indicate which credit bureau reported you as having bad credit, and then you can request a report from that bureau. Credit repair begins with a detailed look at your credit report. Look for any inaccuracies: in some cases, they may be errors in your file, or your credit information may be mistaken for someone else with the same name. If you find any inaccuracies, you can repair your credit by applying in writing to the credit bureau. If you have any supporting documentation, include it, otherwise, simply indicate where the confusion is and request that it be analyzed. This benefits you in two ways: first, if the credit bureau cannot verify the information you are disputing, by default, it must be deleted from your file; second, if the bureau does not respond to your request for investigation within 30 days, the disputed information must be deleted.

If it turns out that your bad credit is the result of an error, you should usually go to the credit bureau; that's all you need to do to repair the credit. When you order your credit report, keep in mind that your processors will make the process seem more difficult than it is, since, in terms of hours, they are not interested in responding to many requests for credit reports.

Step 2. Contact Your Bank Agency

Once you went over your credit report and determined that everything is correct, the next step in repairing your credit history is to contact creditors with whom you have delinquent accounts. You should repair these accounts as soon as possible to successfully repair your credit.

In many cases, the creditor's priority is to recover as much of the account receivable as possible. Many people are surprised at how accommodating they can be in terms of organizing a payment process: in many cases, the creditor will eliminate interest or even reduce the bill and return it for immediate payment. If you can't pay immediately, propose a payment plan for the creditor that you can stick to: Creditors will accommodate most payment proposals because, again, your primary interest will be to recover the debt.

Remember that the reason you're doing this is to repair your credit history, so under no circumstances should you commit to a payment plan with your creditors that you won't be able to meet would only end up making problems worse in the future. If a creditor has repeated issues with a client, it is unlikely that there is much trust in the relationship, so they probably won't want to help you. Instead, choose something you can meet and explain your current financial situation to the creditor. By doing this, you can often achieve credit repair quickly.

Step 3. Try and Avoid the Collection Agency

The worst and last step a creditor will take is to sell your outstanding debt to a collection agency. In terms of credit repair, this is the worst thing that can happen because it means that whomever you owed money to consider your chances of recovering it so low that you are willing to lose some of the debt. In most cases, the creditor sells the debt to the collection agency at a large discount, often half the amount owed.

When a debtor sold his loan to a collection agency, he just "canceled" it and created the lowest possible mark on his credit history. If this happens, try and act as soon as possible after being contacted by the collection agent. Before you negotiate with the collection company, talk to your creditor. See if the creditor will remove the "canceled" mark from your credit history. This is something they will do in exchange for immediate payment.

If your creditor is not interested in negotiating payment, you would be in trouble with the collection agent. It can and will happen that the debt collector stays in a very intimidating and threatening position, usually implying that they are willing to take you to trial. The two points to keep in mind are that the collection company bought your debt for less than the amount owed, and you are unlikely to be sued. Your best solution is to offer to make an immediate payment for less than the actual balance of your debt. Most companies will accept this, usually because making a profit on any payment that exceeds 50% of their debt and offering to pay immediately allows them to close their file and work on other issues. When dealing with a collection agent, only offer full payment as a last resort.

Step 4. Apply for a Secured Credit Card

Credit repair can be a slow process, and you may find yourself building a bit of credit backing slowly over a long time. A good place to start is with a "secured" credit card. These credit cards are issued by banking agencies that generally target people who have bad credit. Unlike a regular credit card, for which you will no doubt be rejected if you have a bad credit score, it is a secured credit; the card usually requires you to give an initial deposit equivalent to the credit limit of the card. That is, you give the company $500 for a card with a credit limit of $500, and they reserve the right to use that deposit against any outstanding balance that remains for too long.

From the issuer's point of view, their bad credit won't matter because they don't take any risk: you'll never owe them more money than you've already given them to start with. From your point of view, secured cards are far from ideal, but if you have bad credit and need to participate in credit repair, you have no choice.

Once you have a secured credit card, use it sparingly but regularly, and make sure to make all your payments on time. By doing this over a long time, you will slowly repair your credit history and regain the confidence of creditors who rejected you in the past.

Step 5. Consider a Company That Specializes in Credit Repair

If you find that none of the above works for you in terms of credit repair, consider going to a company that specializes in this type of process. Many of these companies will offer to "clean up your credit record" for a fee. While the services of a credit repair company can be much more helpful, depending on your situation, you must be very careful to avoid scams and read all the fine print that is in most cases.

The basic strategy of most credit repair companies will be to encourage you to claim absolutely everything on your credit report with your credit bureau. The idea is to flood the office with more requests than they can respond to within 30 days because remember that if the office can't provide documentation for something in your file within 30 days, it must be remote. However, it is questionable how effective this really is, although the office, if it does not document them, it must remove items within 30 days. In most cases, companies will continue to investigate the claims, and when they finally find the proper documentation, the items will be added again.

Whatever you decide regarding a credit repair company, always remember to go over the documents carefully. Also, note that credit repair companies cannot legally accept payments until services are completed. They are also required to clearly describe all payments and terms.

CHAPTER 3:
SECRETS OF CREDIT REPAIR

It is well and good to take care of negative items in your report that are dragging down your credit score. However, what is the point of doing this and then picking up fresh negative items?

Credit repair will take unnecessarily long to implement successfully if you do not overhaul your financial activity. Here are tips that will help you maintain the credit score increases that you worked so hard to achieve.

Tip #1: Draw Up a Budget and Stick to It

If there ever were a rule on keeping the credit on track and generally improving finance, it would read like this: Live within your means.

It may not always be the case, but in some cases, you will find the need to take on a loan because some emergency came up. This is why, no matter how effective you are at making your paycheck stretch out over a month, you should save some money every month so that you do not have to take out credit so frequently, damaging your credit in the process.

Be responsible with your credit card. If you are a typical American with a penchant for whipping out the credit card, your card is likely the major reason behind your poor credit. Avoid making unnecessary purchases with frequency because you get closer to having your card maxed out this way.

Check your account every evening before you go to bed, so you have an idea of how your finances are faring. By and by, and with responsible behavior, you will get closer to an excellent credit score.

Tip #2: Pay All Your Bills on Time

By now, you know that a large portion of your credit score—35%, to be specific—hinges on your payment history. Payment history is not truly emphatic on whether you actually made your payments so much as it is on how timely your payments were. Even one late payment can seriously hurt your credit.

Ensure you know how much you owe in bills each month, and make sure you pay every bill. Even better, why not have an automated system agreed with your bank that will see allowed amounts automatically channeled toward paying off respective bills.

Tip #3: Get Your Secured Credit Card and Use It Responsibly

Be responsible for this card. Remember that the deposit amount you put in also acts as your credit limit. Keep the debt to credit ratio at 30% or below. Otherwise, keep working on increasing the card's credit limit if you figure that you will need to take out larger amounts in the future.

CHAPTER 4:
EFFECTIVE STRATEGIES FOR REPAIRING YOUR CREDIT

Pay-to-Delete Strategy

If you have derogatory items in your credit report, you can opt to pay the credit balance only if the creditor agrees to delete the items from your credit report. Don't agree to a $0 balance appearing on your credit report since this taints your reputation. This will ultimately improve your rating. Actually, the idea is to ensure that, whatever amount you agree to pay, it doesn't show up as your last date of the activity. If the creditor only cares about their money, why should they bother telling the world that you have finally paid?

In most instances, the creditors often write off debts within just 2 years of constant defaulting, after which this information is sold in bulk to a collection company for some pennies of a dollar. This means that the collection companies will even be just fine if you even pay a fraction of what you ought to pay. Whatever you pay, they will still make money! This makes them open to negotiations such as pay-to-delete since they have nothing to lose, anyway.

- Therefore, only use the pay-to-delete approach at this level and not at any other. Actually, the only other way around it for the collection company is a judgment, which can be costly, so you have some advantage here.
- Additionally, use this strategy when new negative items start showing up on your report that could hurt your reputation as a credit consumer.
- Also, since the creditors will often sell the same information to multiple collection companies, you might probably start noting the same debt being reported by several companies; use pay-to-delete to get them off your report.
- You can also use this strategy if you have not been successful in getting items off your credit report using other methods, as opting to go the dispute way might only make the process cyclic, cumbersome, tiresome, and frustrating; you don't want to get into this cycle.

Now that you know when to use this method, understanding how the entire process works is very critical. To start with, ensure that you get an acceptance by writing if they agree to your times; don't pay without the letter! After you agree, allow about 45 days for the next credit report to be given to you by your credit monitoring service. These companies have the legal power to initiate the deletion process, so don't accept anything less, such as updating the balance; it is either a deletion or nothing. If they try to stall the process by saying that they cannot delete the problematic item from your credit report, mention that it will only take about 5 minutes for them to fill the Universal Data Form. Don't worry if one company seems not to agree with your terms since another one will probably show up and will gladly take the offer.

In any case, what do they have to gain if they keep your debt when you are willing to pay? Remember that the records will just be in your files for 7 years, and since 2 years are already past, these companies have no choice; otherwise, you can simply let the 7 years pass! However, don't use this as an excuse for not paying your debts since the creditors can sue you to compel you to pay outstanding amounts. This process aims to ensure that whatever bad experience you have with one creditor doesn't make the others make unfavorable decisions on your part.

Note: Don't be overly aggressive with creditors who have a lot to lose in the process, especially the recent creditors, since they can probably sue you. Your goal is to only be aggressive with creditors that are barred by the statute of limitation from suing you in court. You don't want to find yourself in legal troubles to add to your existing problems. Try and remain as smart as possible and make all the right moves to help you repair your credit at the earliest.

Pay-to-delete isn't the only option available to you; you can use other strategies to repair your credit.

Check for FDCPA (Fair Debt Collection Practices Act) Violations

The law is very clear on what collection agencies can do and what they cannot do as far as debt collection is concerned. For instance:

- They should not call you more than once a day unless they can prove that it was accidentally dialed by their automated systems.
- They cannot call you before 8.00 am or after 9.00 pm.
- They cannot threaten, belittle or yell at you to make you pay any outstanding debts.
- They cannot tell anyone else other than your spouse why they are contacting you.
- The best way to go about this is to let them know that you are recording all their calls.
- They cannot take more money from your account than you have authorized if they do an ACH.

- They are also not allowed to send you collection letters if you have already sent them a cease and desist order.

If you can prove that collection companies violate the law, you should file a complaint with the company and have your lawyer send proof indicating the violations; you can then request that any outstanding debt be forgiven. You need to understand that the law is on your side in such circumstances; actually, if the violations are major, the collection companies could be forced to pay fines of up to $10,000 for these violations.

So, if your debt is significantly lower than this, you could be on your way to having your debt cleared since these companies would rather pay your debt than pay the fine. Look for errors on your credit reports.

Your credit report should be free of errors. Even the slightest thing as reporting the wrong date of last activity on your credit report is enough to damage your credit. If the write-off date is different from what has been reported, you can dispute the entry to have it corrected to reflect the actual status of your credit. However, keep in mind that the CRAs will, in most instances, confirm that the negative entry is correct even if this is not the case, which means that they will not remove the erroneous item.

You must put in efforts to get them on the right track. To get them to comply, you have to inform them that the law requires them to have the preponderance of their systems in place to ensure that these errors do not arise. Therefore, the mere fact of confirming the initial error is not enough; inform them about the notice (summons) and complaint to let them understand that you are serious about the matter. Once they have an idea of your stance, they will put in efforts to do the right thing. The thing is that the CRAs don't want any case to go to court since this could ultimately provide proof that their systems are weak or flawed, which means that they will probably be in some bigger problems.

So try and drive a strong point across so that they understand you mean business. The mere exchange of emails will not do, and you must send them details on how strong your case will be. This will make them understand their position, and they will decide to help you to avoid going to court. This will, in turn, work to your advantage in making them dig deeper into the issue. However, this method will only work if you are certain that an error was actually made. You will also require proof for it, so you cannot simply state that there was an error.

Request Proof of the Original Debt

If you are certain that the credit card has been written off for late payment, likely, the carriers (Capital One and Citibank) cannot find the original billing statements within 30 days, which they are required by the law to respond to.

This, in effect, allows you to have whatever entry you have disputed removed from the credit report as if it never happened.

Another handy approach is to request for the original contract that you signed to be provided to prove that you actually opened that particular credit card in the first instance. As you do this, don't just ask for "verification" since this just prompts the collection agency to "verify" that they actually received a request for collection on an account that has your name on it. Pay the original creditor.

When your debt is sold to collection agencies, you will probably risk having new items showing up on your credit report, which can further hurt your credit rating. However, you can stop that by sending a check with the full payment of any outstanding amount to the original creditor, after which you just send a proof of payment to that collection agency and any other, then request them to delete any derogatory items they have reported from your credit report.

It is always a good idea to be in direct contact with your creditor or creditors. In fact, many of these agencies will be fully equipped to cheat you and will follow through on plans to have your report show bad credit scores. It is up to you to try and remove these "middlemen" and make the payment yourself. You could also agree to pay a portion of the money to the creditor as full payment for the sum (the pay to delete strategy).

Under federal law, if the original creditor accepts any payment as full payment for any outstanding debt, the collection agency has to remove whatever they have reported. This will only work if the original creditor accepts the payment; it is possible for some of the checks you pay to the original creditor to be returned to you.

CHAPTER 5:
HOW TO REMOVE HARD INQUIRIES FROM YOUR CREDIT REPORT

Whenever a potential lender or a creditor asks to look into your credit report, it raises an inquiry with the credit bureau. The same will reflect in your report. There are two types of inquiries, either hard or soft inquiry.

If you apply for a line of credit, and the lender checks your credit report to decide if you are a potential candidate, it is a hard inquiry. A hard inquiry will always show up on your credit report. It will affect your overall credit score. If you apply for a mortgage, credit card, auto loan, or any other form of credit, the lender will check your credit report and score. The lender does this with your permission. They will check your credit report with one or all of the major credit bureaus. Since this inquiry is related to a credit application, they are hard inquiries and will show up in your credit report. And since they show up on your credit report, it will influence your credit score.

Now, let us look at the way hard inquiries affect your credit report. If there are too many hard inquiries about your credit report within a short period, then it is a red flag for potential lenders. Hard inquiries, especially multiple ones, can imply that you are looking to open multiple new accounts. If you start opening multiple accounts, it shows that you are in dire need of funds and that your financial position is not that good. It might also mean that you are overspending. So, it harms your credit report as well as your credit score.

You might be thinking that a person might make multiple inquiries about credit because he/she is shopping for the best deal on loan. Credit rating models do consider this possibility. Most will accommodate multiple inquiries made within a short time frame for a line of credit involving a mortgage or a car loan. Numerous inquiries made about a specific credit product will be treated as a single inquiry and will have a relatively smaller effect on your credit report. Usually, you will not be denied credit because of the number of hard inquiries on your credit report. It is because a hard inquiry is only one of the many factors that are taken into consideration for generating your credit report as well as credit score.

Hard inquiries can stay on your credit report for around two years, but as time passes by, their effect is also reduced. Even if you have several hard inquiries within a short period, this cannot be a reason for disqualifying you for credit by a lender. Your credit histories, as well as the promptness of payments, are the other factors that are taken into consideration before you are either approved or rejected for a loan.

If the hard inquiry in the credit report is accurate, then you cannot have it removed. However, you can dispute a hard inquiry if it was started without your permission or if there was an error. If you notice a hard inquiry from an unfamiliar lender in your credit report, it is something you must look into immediately. It is often a sign of identity theft. So, if you find any inaccurate hard inquiries in your credit report, then you can raise a dispute about them. Upon investigation, if the bureau realizes that the hard inquiry was indeed inaccurate, then it will be removed from your report. When this happens, its effect will also be removed from your credit score.

Managing Inquiries

If you are worried that the hard inquiries are hurting your credit score, then you can take the following steps:

- Be prudent and apply for credit only when needed.
- If you are looking for a specific credit line like a mortgage or auto loan, then you do your rate shopping in a short period.
- Keep checking your credit report regularly to ensure that there are no inaccurate hard inquiries on it.
- Start managing the other important factors that influence your credit score.

If a hard inquiry took place without your approval, then you can remove it from your credit history. If you had no prior knowledge of the hard inquiry made about your credit report or your credit profile, then you have the right to have it removed. At times, you can also get these inquiries removed from the credit report that have been made because you were pressured into accepting an application process that you were not interested in. Here are all the instances of hard inquiries that you can remove from your credit report.

- Any inquiry that was made without your prior knowledge.
- Any inquiry that was made without your consent.
- Any inquiry that was made because you were pressured.
- The number of inquiries in your report exceeds the actual amount made.

If you notice an inaccurate hard inquiry on your credit report, then you can send a letter contacting the appropriate agency for its removal. When you are sending a message for removal, you can send it to the credit bureau as well as the lender. Here are the steps you must follow.

The first step is to send a letter for removal of the credit inquiry to the credit bureau and the lender through a certified mail service. A certified mail will record when the letter was sent as well as received. You can use this record as legal proof in case of any discrepancy. This comes in handy, especially when the receiver denies receiving the letter.

Before you send a notice for the removal of your credit inquiries, you need to notify the lender. You are obligated to notify the lender if you wish to take any legal action. Do not be surprised if the lender is not as responsive as the credit bureau. However, this is one step you must not ignore, and it is the right way to go about getting an inaccurate hard inquiry removed from your report.

While you are sending your letter for removal, please ensure that you attach a copy of your credit report with it. Highlight the discrepancy in the report or any other unauthorized inquiries. A credit bureau will have easy access to your account, but it helps investigators if you send a hard copy.

Please ensure that you are sending the letter to the right authority. If the discrepancy was in a report compiled by Equifax, then it does not make any sense to send a copy of the letter to TransUnion. Here are the addresses of the three major credit bureaus in the U.S.

The process of removal of any negative entry from your credit report is lengthy and time-consuming. So, if you like quick results, this process will be a lesson in patience. It might not seem like a couple of points will make much of a difference to your credit score, but they will soon add up to a significant number if left unchecked. Therefore, it is quintessential that you stay on top of any inquiries you make about the removal of negative entries on your credit report. If you want to improve your credit score and keep it high, ensure that all the entries in your credit report are correct.

Notes: Making multiple hard inquiries within a short period is usually an indication of filing for bankruptcy. Numerous hard inquiries signify that you are running out of funds or have already run out of funds. It also shows that your financial position is highly unstable. If a person is looking for multiple means of credit at the same time for different reasons, it is an indication of bankruptcy. So, if you are making any hard inquiries within a short period, be mindful of this.

CHAPTER 6:
THE BASICS OF CREDIT CARD DEBT AND BANKRUPTCY

People know the basics of credit cards. Once you are approved, you then receive your card and activate it. You can use it for pretty much anything, such as purchasing groceries, clothing, or paying bills. The nice part is that you only have to make the minimum payment every month to keep yourself out of credit card debt. Unfortunately, it is this kind of thinking that often leads people into credit card debt.

Below are some basic points that most people don't realize about credit card debt.

1. Know When Short-Term Loans Make More Sense

Sometimes we need to get some cash or find a way to pay a few bills quickly. Many people turn to credit cards for these reasons. They receive their answer within minutes, and their card will arrive in the mail in about five to seven business days. However, sometimes it is better to go to your bank and talk to a loan advisor instead. If you need a couple of thousand dollars to pay off your medical bills, so they aren't sent to a collection agency, it might be best to take out a short-term loan from your local bank or credit union.

2. Credit Card Debt Can Result in Bad Credit

Paying off your credit cards in a less than timely manner or missing the minimum payment aren't the only things that are going to result in you having bad credit; having credit cards that hold high balances can also increase your chances of bad credit. In fact, you should make sure you always have at least 30 percent of your credit limit available.

While it is almost impossible in today's world, your best chance of keeping yourself from having bad credit is by remaining as free of debt as you possibly can.

3. Owing Is the Easy Part, and the Hard Part Is Paying Credit Cards Back

The reality of life is that you never really know what is going to happen. You could have a job for a couple of decades and then find out that you are randomly laid off due to cutbacks. You could have an illness spike that causes surgery. There are a lot of situations that can cause you to think you can start paying your credit cards every other month so you can make other bills. You could also find yourself struggling to pay the full minimum balance, so you may decide to pay about half of it every month.

Another reason your debt will climb is due to your credit limit increasing. This makes you feel mentally secure about being able to purchase your new couch on your credit card because your limit just increased by $500. However, what you are really doing is creating more credit card debt and causing your minimum monthly payment to increase. On top of this, your interest is going to compound, which makes it increase.

4. You Will Find Yourself Spending More Than You Make

It doesn't matter how responsible you are with credit cards; one of the biggest reasons people find themselves in credit card debt is because they spend more than they make every month. Credit cards are very tempting because they provide you with the thought that you can just pay it back later or make smaller payments on the purchase every month. Although, in reality, you should never spend more than what your monthly income is.

5. Most People Use Credit Cards to Handle Emergencies

It is common for people to tell others that a credit card is only used for emergencies, but do you really keep in mind what a true emergency is? Most people live paycheck to paycheck. Therefore, when they see their checking account balance drop low, and there are several days before their next payday, they will start to think about each purchase they make and wonder if they should use their credit card as it is considered an emergency or a need

6. People Think as Long as They Make The Minimum Payment, They Will Be Fine

In reality, you always want to make sure you pay more than the minimum payment. Think of it this way: if you have a $75 minimum payment, at least 25 percent of what you pay is going to go toward interest and fees. This means that you are really only putting 75 percent of your payment toward paying off your debt. Depending on how much you owe, this could be a low amount. If you aren't careful, you could find yourself going over your credit limit, which means your credit card company will charge you their over-the-limit fee.

Furthermore, only paying the minimum payment is going to take you years to pay off. It really doesn't matter how low you feel your credit limit is versus how high you believe your minimum monthly payment is. It can still take at least a couple of years to pay off your debt, providing you stop using your credit card.

Bankruptcy

Only an organization or individual that is unable to completely honor its financial obligation or make payment to its creditor files for bankruptcy. This goes to say that a bankruptcy filing is a legal course of action taken by a company or person to relieve themselves from debt obligations where all outstanding debt of the company is evaluated and paid from the company's assets. As legal proceeding goes, bankruptcy is carried out to give individuals and businesses freedom from debt they have already incurred and at the same time provide creditors with the opportunity to get their debts paid. It can be said to allow for a fresh start by forgiving debts that cannot be paid and at the same time offering creditors a substantive opportunity to get methods of repayment based on the available assets of a person or business that can be liquidated.

Theoretically, this can mean that the ability to file for bankruptcy can benefit the whole economy by giving businesses and individuals a second chance to have the utmost access to consumer credit and by providing creditors with a reliable measure of debt repayment. Once there is the successful completion of a bankruptcy proceeding, the debtor is to be relieved of their obligation from the debt that has been incurred before filing for bankruptcy. However, it will be on their credit record that such a person had acquired debts before and filed for bankruptcy. This information is going to remain on the record for about seven to ten years, depending on the type of bankruptcy filed.

Types of Bankruptcy

There are two types of bankruptcy.

1. **Debt Discharge.** This is simply the cancellation of debt, thanks to bankruptcy. Based on the Internal Revenue Code, a debtor must add into their gross income the discharge of indebtedness, after which a court must have discharged his/her debt upon meeting all conditions. However, if a debtor should refuse financial counseling, commits a crime, fails to fully explain the loss of his/her assets, provides false information during court proceedings, or basically disobeys the orders of the court, a judge can rightfully refuse to discharge the debt of such a person.
2. **The Payment Plan.** This is a kind of bankruptcy filed, where a debtor and his/her lawyer submit to the court a kind of repayment plan of how the debtor plans to pay off his/her debts in three to five years. This plan is dependent on the debtor's income, food,

and utilities, tax, and healthcare expenses. Should the court approve the plan, the debtor proceeds to make the payments required as stipulated in the plan. If such a debtor is consistent with the payments, the remaining debts will be discharged at the end of the three to five-year period. The payments are made to a trustee from the bankruptcy court that then proceeds to pay the creditors while getting a commission too.

Concerning business, the two types of bankruptcy are:

1. **Reorganization Bankruptcy.** This is a kind of bankruptcy filed meant to help business owners who have serious issues with their business but still have regular income and valuable assets and reorganize the business. The business is allowed to continue its operations with the court's supervision of course. The creditors aren't allowed to interfere with the debtors during the supervision. Business owners will have to share their reorganization plan with the creditors providing them part of the payment. But if the creditors do not agree with the plan, they have the right to file a competing plan.
2. **Farming Bankruptcy.** It is a type of bankruptcy specially designed for farmers of the same family. It is to help the family reorganize their farming business as well as settle all their debts. The unpredictable nature of farming and seasonal moods is factors that are seriously considered.

Implications of Bankruptcy

Before you consider filing for bankruptcy, you need to first understand how it works, as well as the pros and cons. It's not a simple issue that can be done quickly but has a complex side only a bankruptcy attorney understands. It would be best if you find out everything you can before filing for bankruptcy. Find below the consequences of filing bankruptcy.

Pros

1. **Discharge.** Getting debts discharged is one major reason people file for bankruptcy. And when such debt is discharged, erasing all your debts as well as preventing creditors from collecting further payments from you, the debtor becomes relieved. It's one huge advantage of filing for bankruptcy. Not everyone who filed for debt discharge is granted. If you owe debts on alimony, tax liabilities, or child support, filing for bankruptcy would be a waste of time. Such debts are not forgiven nor discharged.

2. **Automatic Stay.** Here is another advantage to being enjoyed when a bankruptcy is filed. It is a situation whereby the person who files for bankruptcy becomes automatically protected from the creditors and the property over the collection of debts. The protection stays until the court finally decrees the debts to be honored and forgiven or discharged. In a situation that involves divorce proceedings, the automatic stay might be lifted.

Cons

1. **Loss of Property.** There's a possibility that a bankruptcy filer might lose his/her property if the court decides it's valuable enough to pay off the debt owed. This could happen if you include your property in your case to the bankruptcy trustee. Your creditor could have higher leverage in trying to get your property, especially if you used such property initially as collateral.
2. **Credit Score.** Another downside to filing for bankruptcy is that it decreases your credit score. Loaners will only see you as risky when they check your credit history because filing for bankruptcy won't in any way clean up your debt history even though your debt is canceled. However, it's a better option than acquiring debt. You can always rebuild your credit score later.
3. **Privacy.** If you're sensitive about your privacy, filing for bankruptcy might not be for you, and this explains why you must do your research if you want to file for bankruptcy. You can either prepare yourself against the consequences or look for other options. When you file a bankruptcy case, every detail about your financial statements becomes public. In other words, anyone can access your personal information without your permission. The amount you owed, who your creditors were, and your bankruptcy schedule can be assessed easily by anyone. It can be such a big deal if you cherish your privacy.

CHAPTER 7: CONTROLLING VARIOUS KINDS OF DEBT

Common Types of Debt

It depends on how you choose to see this. There are different kinds or types of debts. We will cut them into four groups to make this fun. Now, the first group.

1. Secured and Unsecured Loans

Secured Loans

Secured loans are the types of debts you get by offering something as surety in case you don't pay that money up. As an example, if you are buying a house, a car, or getting a big work machine, you may opt for a loan when you don't have enough funds to clear the bills yourself. Often, that is a lot of money, and your credit company wants to be sure you're paying it all without complications. So, you are asked to mortgage some of your valued assets in turn. They keep the documents until your payment is complete. If you don't pay up, there are a few legal actions to make, and they sell the assets. The norm is that you take this type of loan on significant investments.

Unsecured Loans

Unsecured loans are the direct opposite of secured loans. You do not have to stake anything to access a loan like this. All you need is to indicate your interest, submit your essential documents, and the loan is yours. The type of loan you're asking for is what determines what you will be offering. For example, your credit report may be enough to get you another credit card. You may have to drop a little deposit plus your credit report when you're signing up for some utilities. All of these have a small or minimal risk for the user. Only that you can cover simple services with this type of loan, no more. Now, you can imagine which weighs higher on a credit score ranked by FICO.

2. Fixed and Revolving Payment Method

Fixed Payment Method

A lot of times, your credit company lays out clear terms, duration, and method of payment to you. When this happens, we say you have got a fixed payment method. Usually, fixed payment methods attract fixed interests too. When you take part in a dealership deal, for example, you may be graced to get that money paid at a particular amount each month and a particular interest rate. Say the car is worth a thousand USD. You are allowed to pay up in two years, with a total interest of 30%. That is pretty straightforward, right? That's just how fixed payment loans work. A mortgage is an example of fixed payment loans, so you might say they are pretty standard.

Revolving Payment Method

These types of loans are those that swing like unpredictable bells. There are no exact modalities on most items. You simply take the loans and pay as you can. For example, you can pay when you have the funds; there is no exact deadline for payments. You don't get a limit to interest rates too. Often, your utility, as well as your credit card, fall into this category. This is the exact reason you draw up a credit card, and you can use the credit card as much as you like each month. You don't have to pay up that money when the month ends. You can pay a little now, a lot more over the coming months. But as FICO had earlier advised, it makes perfect sense to draw up only 30% or less of your credit limits. Expectedly, your interest rate is determined by how promptly you clear off that debt.

3. Good and Bad Loans

No questions; this list can't be closed if this group isn't here.

The Good Loans

Classifying loans as good or bad does not exist in official records. Maybe if it did, nobody would ever be excited to try out the bad ones. In any case, a right loan is any loan drawn to invest in resources that may become useful and available over a long period, sometimes, forever. Some of them are:

- ***Mortgage***. If it is damning to size up your mortgage and you are planning to hand over the building, my sincere suggestion is that you keep pulling through, and you remain upbeat. This is one of the loans you can't ever regret taking. It is glaring to anyone that houses are assets that you don't use up any moment soon. A home may get into a bad shape sometimes. That's normal. You are expected to keep it brimming with brightness naturally. If you do things right, you can't ever have to pay rents. You also have an asset you can risk getting considerable loans to build your career. If things get worse, you can auction the house and restart your careers somewhere. However, you choose to see it, a loan drawn to get a home is a good one. Just be sure you can keep paying till the end before drawing the loan at all.
- ***Student Loans***. Well, you might hear someone say drawing student loans is insane. But if you look over the sayings, you'd have something different. You've got to get a good education, and

you can't afford it at that moment. It makes perfect sense to tangle yourself in a loan, bag that degree, and pay back much more quickly. As you may fear, your first few years after school would be spent clearing your old debt. But you become free soon, and you'd have access to opportunities you may not have found without top training. From all viewpoints, you see this, it is a win-win for all teams. So, I'd vote this as a right loan!

- ***Business***. Now, this is another perspective. If you are getting the loans to jack up your investments, you are settling for a good one too. It is undoubtedly a risk since the business may pick up and may not. But if you probably play your cards right, your business can boom, and that is the start of a goal you didn't see coming.

So, Bad Loans?

- ***Auto Loans***. For a fact, you must be curious to know why auto loans should be tagged a bad debt, isn't it? I bet! Well, it is. Auto loans, dealerships, and whatever kind of car loan you get into is a bad loan. This is because cars are not assets that can be used for a long while. If you sign a two or five-year loan deal, your car is already developing some sorts of problems. So, you'd have to spend on it, and at that same time, pay your auto loans. It would be a mess in a few years.
- ***Credit Card Loans***. Credit Card Loans are probably the worst you can take. They can't be used to get important stuff. And either you take note or not, your debt is on the rise with every month you forgot to clear up.
- ***Most Other Loans***. Most of the other types of loans fall into this category, especially those you draw from friends and family. They are often not precisely significant and should be avoided. Except, of course, they are critical to you, and you are sure there's some way you can quickly pay it all back.

How to Control Your Credit

Regardless of what credit types you have drawn, it is vital to monitor and control it all before it gets out of hand. Even if it's slipped a bit, the best option you've got is to find some way to monitor and control it. Hence, I'll be showing you some easy and practical ways in the next few lines:

Don't Let Things Slip off. That's the first rule. Prevention is way better than cure. It stands to reason that if you can plan appropriately and watch out for sinking moments, you shouldn't have to fight to save your credit score fiercely.

All you need is to do the math. Where are you heading to? What are your chances of hitting it big or terribly crashing? What would you have to do to avoid falling into a debt pit and struggling to pay up? Several things we might say. Your first job is to find those targets and set them working.

Don't Spend Payments. Pending payments only increase your penalties. Whether for fixed and revolving debts. So, with the facts that you should avoid pending your payments. Clear them off the instant you can.

Don't Toy With Revolving Debts. Revolving debts are full of surprises. You would usually assume they are the littlest, and so, they can be paid after the much bigger debts. In reality, your revolving debts (like your credit cards) cart away more than your fixed debts. They tend to increase all the time, and there's a high potential for interest increase too, which doesn't happen in fixed credit cases. Hence, it washes that you should pay them up before considering some other debts at all. Don't delay others too!

If you do the math and your revolving debts are out, you will have a concrete idea of how to tackle the only other debts you have left. This itself is an acute style of controlling debts that you didn't notice. Now you know, cheers.

CHAPTER 8: CONSEQUENCES OF NOT PAYING OFF YOUR DEBT

What happens when you go into serious delinquency or default on your loans? Well, it depends on the type of loan. With cars and houses, they can be repossessed by the bank. With consumer debt, you are often going to have to declare bankruptcy to wipe out old debts if you are far enough underwater.

Government-backed student loans, however, are a whole different beast. They can NOT be removed via bankruptcy. After 270 days of no payments, they are officially in default and sit there like a bad acne breakout on your credit report, making your score look yucky. Some student loan companies will then turn the loans over to official debt collection companies, which start yammering your phone away about late payments. Besides, you'll be on the hook for their own special fees. Yay.

You might have to try the 'secured credit card' trick to build up your credit again after this kind of financial disaster. Some people want to reach out to a debt settlement company or try to get a payday loan, but please don't! Debt settlement companies have to get paid too, you know? And they'll come after your money one way or another. Most of them are scams. The only honest ones are nonprofits, and even those are doubtful. Payday loans charge sickening interest rates of more than 500% in some cases, so for a $1,000 payday loan, you'll be screwed out of more than $5,000. What kind of sense does that make? Stay far away from them.

If you don't pay your credit cards, they sit untouched with the original creditor for about six months. An original creditor is a bank like Chase, Citi, Capital One, Discover, or American Express. If you keep making payments, even if it's just $10 a month, the account will remain open with the original creditor.

But if you stop making payments for six months, then the original creditor turns the debt along with its collected interest over to a debt collection company. They then attempt to collect the debt for another six months. By now, you've not made a single payment for a year. If no payments are made, then your debt, with any added fees and other expenses from the debt collection company, is then turned over to a law office, where a judgment is brought against you in the form of a lawsuit. The law office represents either the original creditor or the debt buying company. The amount of small claims lawsuits based on collecting past debts has increased significantly in the past ten years, and now there are specialty law firms devoted solely to debt collecting from ordinary people. Well, at least we don't have debtors' prisons anymore.

If this happens, the creditor or debt collector is the plaintiff, and you become the defendant. You can even go to trial and meet with a lawyer to set up court-ordered payment plans based on the actual financial paperwork that you bring to the courthouse. Keep in mind that there is often interest included even after judgment is brought against you.

If you still fail to pay, a lien could be put on your property, and your wages could be garnished from your current paycheck. It's legal in most states to garnish up to 25% of your wages. However, if you are seriously buried, you should know that the great state of Texas does not allow wage garnishment, so if you are considering a move, Texas might be the place!

Being informed about this entire process will help you make better decisions on repairing your credit before bills go to collections. Dealing with debt collectors is its own game, so let's take a look. It's a bit different than just dealing with a credit card company. The rules have changed.

Make Debt Collectors Go Away

Unfortunately, debt collector companies just won't take your word for it that you're going through a rough time or that they need to leave you alone. They do need to see proof. Collectors love paperwork! The more proof in writing, the better. So, before calling up your debt collector to give them the complete story of why you can't pay, get yourself prepared.

Spend the time gathering up all of your financial paperwork. Get copies of your taxes that show your income and your financial situation. Gather your doctor's bills, your SSDI paperwork, your paystubs, and, if you're sharing an income or living on someone else's SSI, all the paperwork that goes along with that person.

Then, once you've gathered all your paperwork, call up your collector. Keep an eye on the prompts on the phone until you get to the customer service department. Be prepared to wait a long time on the phone. Just set aside the time to devote to this. Be polite but brief and direct. Tell the representative that you can't pay and you have the proof you can't. Ask them how you can get them the paperwork so they can attach it to your file. Maybe you can send it in an email as a PDF attachment or mail it or fax it to them? Get the name of the representative and the state (or country) where they are. Take down your account number. Ask if you need to provide any other paperwork as proof of the inability to pay. If they tell you that you need something, comply with that. Ask if they can put a financial hardship status on your account. If so, that's great. Many collectors don't.

After you hang up, immediately follow the representative's instructions to send the paperwork to the collector. Keep all originals and only send copies. Put a note in your calendar to call in two weeks to follow up.

After two weeks, call up the customer service department again. Explain that you spoke to "Name" and ask if have they received all of your paperwork. Make sure every last piece of paper is attached to your file.

The third step is to put your name on their "Do Not Call" list. VERY IMPORTANT: Keep in mind that they won't call about important stuff, either, like courtesy calls notifying you that your balance has changed. So, do this with caution. Yes, the phone calls are uber annoying. But that's the primary legal way of contacting you.

You actually need to send your request to not be contacted in writing. Write or type legibly on a blank sheet of paper:

To Capital One,

Please put my name on your "Do Not Call" list. Please remove my name from all call lists. I understand that I will not receive any phone calls.

Thank you,

Your Name

Keep a copy in case you need it for legal purposes. After you've mailed your request to the collector, wait three weeks for them to receive it and attach the request to your file. Your account will be flagged "Do Not Call" if it's been done properly. Follow up and call the collector to make sure your account has been flagged. Ask the representative if you need to do anything else to make sure you are not contacted.

Throughout this whole negotiating process, continue to send what payments you can. Yes, you can absolutely send small payments to a debt collector, even if it's just $10 or $20 a month. It buys you a little time to change your financial situation. Don't give up, and don't just stop sending payments.

You can also settle with debt collectors. Ask them about settlement options and start with less than 50% of the debt owed. They might come back with a counter-offer. After you agree to the settlement, stick with its terms to the letter, or you will be on the hook for the whole amount, and you can't renegotiate for a new settlement. If you do this, make sure you have them put Paid in Full on your credit report if possible.

If your financial situation changes at any point (you get on SSI, you lose a job), or you move, then notify your debt collector immediately. Make sure the proper paperwork is attached to your file, and your address is correct. You'd be surprised at how much incorrect information can get attached to your account.

CHAPTER 9: CREDIT BUREAUS (TRANSUNION, EQUIFAX, AND EXPERIAN)

The ideal approach to manage your credit capably and assume responsibility for your financial circumstance is to be educated. This takes a brief period and exertion on your part. Yet, since your credit scores are so crucial to dealing with your accounts and setting aside cash, you must know as much as you can regarding the credit bureaus that formulate credit appraisals. To assist you with getting a running beginning on that strategy's, there are some details on TransUnion, Experian, and Equifax, the primary credit bureaus of the U.S.:

TransUnion

TransUnion has workplaces over the nation that manage various parts of credit: identity theft, credit management, and other credit issues; and also types of credit customers, for example, personal, business, and press inquiries. If you find errors on your TransUnion credit report, you can call them at 800.916.8800 or visit their site to debate them. If that you believe that you are a casualty of identity theft, call them at 800.680.7289 at the earliest opportunity.

Experian

Like other credit bureaus, Experian provides a wide range of various administrations for people, businesses, and the media. Experian is based in Costa Mesa, CA, and has a website. Yet, if you discover errors in your report or need to report potential identity theft, this credit bureau makes it elusive to telephone numbers on the site. Instead, they encourage guests to utilize online forms for questions, identity theft reports, and different issues.

Equifax

Based in Atlanta, GA, Equifax likewise has various departments to help people with multiple types of questions and concerns. Their website is additionally set up to have people utilize online forms to work on errors, report identity theft, and handle different matters. In any case, if somebody believes that their identity has been taken, the individual in question can, however, call 888.397.3742 to report it to Equifax. If that somebody detects a blunder on their Equifax credit report, that person must utilize the contact number on the story to question it. There is no number on the site to describe errors.

These are the three credit bureaus in the nation, and they each adopt an alternate strategy to enabling people to get in touch with them to pose inquiries or address any issues they might be encountering. Rather than reaching the credit bureaus legitimately, numerous people prefer to utilize a credit checking administration to assist them with dealing with their credit and stay over their funds. The credit bureaus all have related projects; however, most people prefer to utilize an independent organization to assist them with these issues. That way, they get an impartial perspective on their credit score and a lot more devices to manage and improve their credit ratings proactively.

Dealing With Credit Bureaus

Today, where the economy is at its weak point, having good credit is a necessary tool. This is because it allows you to obtain house loans, car loans, credit cards, and other convenient financial services and instruments. You may be able to live without having good credit. You can discern the credit bureau that holds your file by looking at any rejection letter you received from a recent credit application. If you are dealing with the credit bureau that handles your data, keep in mind that it belongs in the business of collecting and selling information. As such, you should not provide them with any detail, which is not necessarily legal. When you already have your credit report, make sure to check for any errors or discrepancies. If you find anything that is questionable in your story, you can send the credit bureau a written request for them to investigate the failure. In general, the credit bureau has the burden of documenting anything that is included in your credit report. If the credit bureau fails to investigate the error or neglects your request for an investigation within 30 days, the error should be removed. You need to educate yourself about the legal obligations of credit bureaus to have a successful credit repair process. Before dealing with them, make sure you know all the legal aspects so you would not end up paying for something that should not be charged with a fee. Remember, credit bureaus are also businesses and that they own many credit repair companies.

Making the Best of Credit Bureaus

It is a little annoying to learn that all three credit bureaus have sensitive financial data. However, there is no method to prevent lenders and collection entities from sharing your information with the above companies. You can limit any possible problems associated with the credit bureaus by evaluating your credit reports annually and acting immediately in case you notice some errors. It is also good to monitor your credit cards and other open credit products to ensure that no one is misusing the accounts. If you have a card that you do not often use, sign up for alerts on that card so that you get notified if any transactions happen and regularly review statements for your active tickets. Next, if you notice any signs of fraud or theft, you can choose to place a credit freeze with the three credit bureaus and be diligent in tracking the activity of your credit card in the future.

How the Bureaus Get Their Information

To learn how the score gets calculated, first, we need to learn about all the different inputs of your score, aka where the bureaus get their info. You may have many factors that report information to the credit bureaus or none. Credit cards are called revolving accounts or revolving debt by the credit bureaus. Each monthly payment and balance are reported, as well as any late payments. This means that any cards that have your name on them will also report to all the bureaus. This includes cards that belong to a spouse or parent. If you are an authorized user on the account, it gets reported on your credit no matter what. Many people have their credit ruined by a spouse or parent going into bankruptcy or not paying their credit card bills. If your name is on any credit card that belongs to people that may not pay their bills, ask them to take your name off immediately! Installment loans also report information to the credit bureaus. If you went down to your local Sears and financed a washer/dryer set by putting up a down payment, that is an installment loan. The details of these loans are all reported; the total balance, as well as the timeliness and amounts of your monthly payments. If you have mortgages or student loans, that information does get reported. Total amounts due, total paid so far, and the status of monthly payments is all reported. This information is kept track of and organized in their databases.

CHAPTER 10: HOW TO PAY OFF DEBT

Start Eliminating High-Interest Debts First

When you are trying to eliminate your credit card debt, the biggest obstacle that will stand in your way is the ones that carry a very high rate of interest. Sometimes, the rate of interest can even be in double-digits, sometimes as high as 22%. In that case, paying it off can be a really difficult task. But the reason why I am asking you to start eliminating them first is that when you have cleared these debts, you will have a greater amount of money left in your hand at the end of each month.

Another thing that you could do, but only if you have enough credit available, is to apply for a new credit card. But this should be a zero-interest one. Once you get it, transfer the balance to eliminate the high-interest debt. Yes, I know that some of you might be thinking that it is not a sensible thing to do to apply for another credit card, and that is why I will be asking you to get it only if you think you have enough self-restraint not to buy a bunch of stuff that you don't need.

Keep Making Small Payments

Quite contrary to the technique I mentioned above is another technique which is called the snowflake technique. With this process, you will be making small payments towards your debt every time you get some extra cash in hand. Whatever payment you are making, it does not matter as long as you keep paying.

You can pay $10, or you can pay $20, but at the end of the year, you will find that you have reduced about $1000 simply by paying such small amounts almost every day, even if you are paying $2 on any day.

People often ignore this method, thinking that it will be only small amounts, but you should not make the mistake of overlooking these small amounts as they have quite the power in them. When you are making these small payments, it would feel as if they are not even leaving any dent, but they will sum up and cause a considerable effect on your debt with time.

Preventive Measures to Avoid Credit Card Debt

Have an Emergency Fund

Think about a situation when you have encountered a problem that requires you to spend a lot of money, for example, a car repair or job loss, or medica emergencies. In such a situation, what you need is an emergency fund, but when people don't have that, they resort to credit cards for help.

But why arrive at such a situation when you can build an emergency fund that will cover at least six months' expenses. If you are finding it difficult to come up with a huge amount, then start by accumulating $500 and then work your way up to $1000. A fund of this size will help you to figure out any small expenses that crop up overnight. Take your time to build your emergency fund so that you do not have to rely on debt ever.

But Only Those Things That You Can Afford

When you have a credit card in hand, it can get really tempting, and you start buying whatever you think you want. But take a step back and think about whether you can really afford that item if you did not have a credit card. If not, then don't buy it now. Make a goal to save the money required for purchasing that item instead of buying it on credit.

Don't Transfer Balance If Not Necessary

Some people have this habit of clearing their balance with a higher credit card, but such repeated balance transferring can actually backfire on you. When you keep transferring balanced without keeping track of your activities, you might end up with an ever-increasing balance, and you will also have to clear the fee requires for all those transfers.

Try Not Taking Out a Cash Advance

Sometimes, you may be in the moment, and you were not thinking clearly, so you decide to take a cash advance. But you have to remember and remind yourself that a cash advance comes with very hefty transaction fees, and you are not even going to get a grace period in which you can avoid the charges. Moreover, you will have to realize that you are getting into credit card debt if you have started taking cash advances. The moment you see it happening, you will have to start working on that emergency fund and also tweak your budget.

Lastly, I would like to say that no matter how many measures you take, try avoiding increasing your credit cards unnecessarily because the more the number of credit cards, the more you will have to stop yourself from overspending.

CHAPTER 11:
FCRA AND OTHER LAWS

The Fair Credit Reporting Act gives you the right to:

- Know the name, address, and phone number of anyone who has seen your credit record over the past two years for employment purposes and the right to know who has reviewed your credit information for any other purpose over the past 12 months
- Have a credit bureau notify employers who reviewed your credit record over the past two years or anyone else who may have reviewed your file over the previous six months, of any corrections or deletions made to your credit file, if you so request and provide the credit-reporting agency with the names of all companies and individuals you want to be notified
- Have a brief explanatory statement added to the credit file concerning information in your file that you dispute but have been unsuccessful in changing or deleting
- To have a bankruptcy deleted after ten years
- Be notified by a company that it has requested an investigative report on you

The CARD Act of 2009

The role the CARD Act of 2009 plays in credit repair is indirect in nature. Rather than giving you a mechanism for challenging the credit-reporting agencies, it acts as "preventative medicine" by guaranteeing you equitable treatment and some ability to control their own destiny. In short, the act will make it less likely for you to get into credit card debt because of abusive practices by credit card issuers. Below, I list the key provisions of the act.

Stops Surprise Rate Increases and Changes in Terms

- No more indiscriminate interest rate hikes or universal default on your credit card simply because you were late on another debt
- If your rate is increased for cause (such as 60-day delinquency), the credit card company must review your payment record periodically and adjust the rate to its previous level if you have made your payments on time for six months
- Credit card issuers cannot increase your rates in the first year

- Promotional rates are permitted but must remain in force for a minimum of six months
- Rates and terms may be changed, but a 45-day notice is required

Prohibits Unnecessary Fees

- Card issuers are no longer permitted to charge you a fee to pay a credit card debt by mail, telephone, or electronic transfer, the exception being live services to make rush payments
- Over the limit, fees are banned unless you choose to allow the issuer to complete over-limit transactions, and even if you do, the act limits these fees to one per billing cycle
- Charges must be reasonable and proportional to the transgression
- Improved protection against exorbitant fees on the low limit, high-fee credit cards

Requires Consumer-Oriented Application and Timing of Card Payments

- If you pay more than your minimum payment, the excess must be applied first to the credit card balance with the highest rate of interest (typically the cash advance balance)
- Card issuers cannot set early morning deadlines for payments
- Statements must be mailed twenty-one days before the due

No More "Double-Cycle" Billing

- Stops the dubious practice of basing finance charges on the average balance over two billing cycles, which penalizes you if you pay your balance in full
- Prohibits late fees caused by delays in crediting your payment
- Payments made at local branches must be credited same-day
- Mandates that credit card companies evaluate your ability to pay before issuing your credit card or raising your credit limit

Requires Improved Disclosure of Credit Terms and Conditions

- Mandates that you be given 45 days' notice of interest rate, fee, and finance charge increases

- Disclosures must be provided upon your card's renewal if terms have changed
- Credit card companies must disclose the length of time to retire your debt and total interest expense that results from making only the minimum payment
- Each billing statement must disclose payment due dates and applicable late payment fees

Makes Industry Practices More Transparent

- Card issuers must make their credit card agreements available on the Internet and furnish those agreements to the Federal Reserve Board, which will also publish them on their website
- The Federal Reserve Board is required to review the consumer credit card market, the terms of credit card agreements, the practices of credit card issuers, and the cost and availability of credit to consumers
- Mandates the Federal Trade Commission to prevent the deceptive marketing of so-called free credit reports

Precludes the Exploitation of Young People

- Persons under the age of twenty-one must prove their ability to pay or provide a co-signer aged 21 or older to or their credit card application will not be approved
- Limits prescreened offers of credit to persons under 21 years of age
- Credit limit increases on co-signed accounts must also be approved by the person jointly responsible for the debt

Provides for Higher Penalties

- Implements more severe penalties for any company violating the Truth in Lending Act for credit card customers

Gift Card Rules

- Mandates that gift cards be valid for five years and eliminates the practice of graduated reductions in card value and hidden fees

Protects Entrepreneurs

- The Federal Reserve is required to study the use of credit cards by small businesses and make recommendations for regulatory and legislative changes
- The act establishes Small Business Information Security Task Force to address the information technology security needs of small business and develop measures to prevent the loss of credit card data

Mandates Financial Literacy

- Mandates the development of a comprehensive plan to improve financial literacy education and the summarization of existing financial literacy initiatives
- It is always a good idea to attach a copy of your credit report with any correspondence you send to a credit-reporting agency with the error(s) highlighted or circled.
- Avoid including anything in your correspondence that is unprofessional or frivolous in nature. The credit reporting agencies can reject frivolous disputes. However, the credit-reporting agency must inform you in writing of their refusal to investigate and include an explanation of why it views your request as frivolous or irrelevant. Maintaining a business-like approach will add credibility to your allegations of inaccuracies.

CHAPTER 12: WHAT IS SECTION 609

What Is 609?

Basically, a 609 is known as a dispute letter, which you would send to your creditor if you saw you were overcharged or unfairly charged. Most people use a 609 letter to get the information they feel they should have received. There are several reasons why some information might be kept from you.

A 609 letter is sent after two main steps: first, you see that the dispute is on your credit report. Second, you have already filed and processed a debt validation letter. The basis of the letter is that you will use it to take unfair charges off of your credit report, which will then increase your credit score.

The 609 letters can easily help you delete your bad credit. Other than this, there are a couple of other benefits you will receive from the letter. One of these benefits is that you will obtain your documentation and information as the credit bureau has to release this information to you. Secondly, you will be able to obtain an accurate credit report, which can definitely help you increase your credit score.

There are also disadvantages to the 609 letters. One of these disadvantages is that collection agencies can add information to your credit history at any time. A second disadvantage is that you still have to repay debt. You cannot use the 609 letters to remove the debt you are obligated to pay. Finally, your creditor can do their own investigation and add the information back into your credit report, even if it was removed (Irby, 2019).

One of the reasons 609 came to be is because one of five people state they have inaccurate information on the credit report (Black, 2019). At the same time, many people believe that this statistic is actually higher than 20% of Americans.

How 609 Works to Repair Bad Credit

If you notice anything on your report that should not be there, you need to use the 609 loopholes to file a dispute, which could result in their wrong information being taken off of the report. If this is the condition, your credit score will increase as you will no longer have this negative inaccuracy affecting your score.

How to File a Dispute With 609

It is important to note that there are several template letters for 609. What this means is that you can easily download and use one of these templates yourself. While you usually have to pay for them, there are some which are free. Of course, you will want to remember to include your information in the letter before you send it.

You will want to make sure everything is done correctly as this will make it more likely that the information will come off and no one will place it back on your report again.

1. Find a Dispute Letter Through Googling "609 Dispute Letter"

While you might be able to search for a free download, for some, you will be able to copy and paste into Microsoft Word or onto a Google Doc.

2. Make the Necessary Changes to the Letter

This will include changing the name and address. You will also want to make sure your phone number is included. Sometimes, people include their email addresses, but this is not necessary. In fact, it is always safer to only include your home address or PO Box information. You will also want to make sure to edit the whole letter. If something does not match up to what you want to say in your letter, such as what you are trying to dispute on your credit report, you need to state this. These letters are quite generic, which means you need to add in your own information.

3. You Want to Make Sure That All of Your Account Information You Want to Be Taken off Your Credit Report Is Handwritten

You also want to make sure you use blue ink rather than black. On top of this, you do not need to worry about being too neat, but you want to make sure they can read the letters and numbers correctly. This is an important part of filing your dispute letter because handwritten ones in blue ink will not be pushed through their automated system. They have an automatic system that will read the letter for them and punch in the account number you use. They will then send you a generic letter that states these accounts are now off your credit report, which does not mean that it actually happened. When you write the information down, a person needs to read it and will typically take care of it. Of course, this does not mean that you will not be pushed aside. Unfortunately, this can happen with any letters.

4. You Want to Make Sure That You Prove Who You Are With Your Letters

While this is never a comfortable thing to do, you must send a copy of your social security card and your driver's license, or they will shred your letter. You also need to make sure that you get each of your letters notarized. You can typically do this by visiting your county's courthouse.

5. You Can Send as Many Letters as You Need to

However, keep in mind that the creditor typically will not make you send more than four. This is because when you threaten to take them to court in the third letter, they will realize that your accounts and demands just are not worth it. First, you could damage their reputation, and secondly, you will cost them more money than simply taking the information off of your credit report will.

6. You Will Want to Make Sure That You Keep All Correspondence They Send You

This will come in handy when they try to make you send more information or keep telling you that they cannot do anything. You mustn't give up. Many people struggle to get them to pay attention because that is just how the system works. Therefore, you need to make sure that you do not listen to their quick automatic reply that your information is off of your credit report. You also want to make sure to wait at least three months and then re-run your credit report to make sure the wrong information has been removed. Keep track of every time you need to re-run your credit report as you can use this as proof if they continue to send you a letter stating the information is off of your credit report.

It is important to note that you can now file a dispute letter online with all three credit bureaus. However, this is a new system, which means that it does come with more problems than sending one through the mail. While it is completely your choice whether you use a form to file your 609 dispute or send a letter, you always want to make sure you keep copies and continue to track them, even if you don't hear from the credit bureau after a couple of months. It will never hurt to send them a second letter or even a third.

CHAPTER 13:
HOW TO WRITE A CREDIT REPAIR LETTER 609 THAT WORKS

Writing the Dispute Letter

Removing adverse information from your credit report is the most vital step when trying to improve your score on a short-term basis.

Credit reporting agencies (CRAs) are not obligated to give notification when adverse information is being reported about you. Upon receiving your information, the CRAs' only job under the law is to use their "reasonable procedures" to validate accuracy.

However, there is no proper and detailed explanation of these procedures, like a list of what must be performed. Of course, if the CRAs were legally required to corroborate every piece of information they receive, they will burn out and shut down.

The Disputing Process

The first thing you need to know is that all three credit reporting agencies have to contest the inaccurate information independently. The disputed appearance may be on all three credit reports or may not. Keep in mind that customers may not belong to all credit reporting agencies. This is why you will see that some of the investors are not on the others on one list.

Even though all three credit reporting agencies have the same information, this does not mean that if an item comes out of one credit report, it will come out of the others. No promise is provided what the outcome will be. That is why you have to refute any inaccurate information about each particular article.

They can use their appeal forms when disputing with credit reporting agencies, write your own message, or challenge the item online on their Website. If you decide to dispute by letter writing, simply state the facts in simple, concise sentences.

If you've found more than four entries on your credit report that you need to dispute, don't dispute everything in one letter. Whether you're writing a letter, filling out their form or answering via the Internet, break your disputes. You send or go back every 30 days to the website of the credit reporting agency and challenge up to four more things. Don't overshoot that number. If you have to challenge less than four things, go ahead and dispute the remaining entries. Extend the spacing of conflicts for 30 days.

On submitting each address, expect to receive a revised credit report about 45 days after you send your letter or disagreement online. If your new credit report has not been issued before it's time to appeal the second time, go ahead and mail your second letter or challenge online instead.

Once all the grievance letters have been mailed or posted to their website, and all the revised credit reports have been received, check whether products have been omitted or incomplete. If you need to do the procedure again for the remaining items, space 120 days from your most recent update to the next round of disputes.

CRAs Verification Forms

The FCRA tries to balance the game for consumers with the dispute process.

The dispute process gave the CRAs so much work, so they opted to restructure their dispute process—so they designed and provided a dispute form for consumers and separate verification forms for their source creditors.

Unsurprisingly, completing and returning verification forms are easier for creditors. Moreover, because the CRAs have 30 days to answer your dispute, either to verify or correct an item, creditors are given a few weeks to return the CRAs the verification forms. However, bear something in mind: not every source creditor will turn around these forms within the allotted period—some will not even return them at all. Just because of this, several disputes will bring about items being corrected or deleted.

Fill-In Dispute Forms

Below is an example of multiple-choice dispute options:

[ ] The account/item is not mine.

[ ] The account status is incorrect.

[ ] The account/item is too old to be included in my report.

When trying to initiate a dispute using the online platform, a pop-up may come to ask you if you want to dispute an item. Just select "yes" to continue.

This is just a protection clause used by the CRAs to trick you into thinking that it is illegal to dispute an item the CRAs consider as valid or correct.

Scale through their scare tactic and do not be intimidated. Just know that it is under the law for you to dispute any inaccurate information or item.

If you requested for your reports to be sent via email, among the documents will be a dispute form. The CRAs will advise filling this already typed form only if there are any inaccuracies on your report. The funny thing is that these mailed dispute forms are simpler to complete because of two reasons:

1) Broadcasting their conformity to the legally required dispute process gives them more acclaim.

2) Supplying their forms is more convenient for them—because, with these simplified forms, their trained agents can swiftly read and convey the information on to their creditor verification forms.

If you have simple disputes (listed in a box or a line on the form), you can either use the online or mailed disputes forms. However, if your issues are complex or lengthy and cannot fit into the allotted space or there are not enough options on the document to address all your dispute issues, you may need to write the CRAs.

Concerning the mailed fill-in dispute forms, be cautious when filling them out as they may ask you to give out more personal information to the CRAs than you need to. The CRAs asking for more information does not mean you have to provide it. Just remember that if a fill-in dispute form does not adequately help your case, the best course of action is to write your letter.

How to Write Your Own Dispute Letter

After organizing all your items, you can write your letter, but make sure to put your disputes in one correspondence. It does not matter if you have a long list of disputes. You can arrange your disputes on multiple pages and in different ways.

For instance, in the left column, list all your accounts; in the right column, list the issues in a few words ("not my account," "always paid on time/never late," etc.). Alternatively, you explain your dispute first, then list the accounts associated with the issue. For example, "the following accounts do not belong to me. . ." Just keep it short and straightforward.

When disputing an item with the bureaus you want to be sure that you have a valid reason and are requesting the correct items to be investigated.

Making sure that you are airtight in your dispute reasoning is important.

You will find that dispute reasons will add validity to your future disputes. If you choose to hire an attorney to pursue legal actions, the letters submitted may be called to be used in court.

Do yourself a favor and make sure you are using real dispute instructions with real reasoning behind them. What is meant by this is that you want to make sure that if you are disputing an account and you do not have solid proof that it is reporting inaccurately or in error, then leave some room to be wrong. If you come out and say - THIS ACCOUNT ISN'T MINE, then you are lying and are committing fraud (don't do that).

Sending Your Dispute Letter

When correcting information on your credit report, make sure it reflects with all three CRAs. Even when one or two reports do not show an error appearing on the other, be on the safe side by telling all of them about the error. Do it because the error might be a recent one and has yet to spread to other reports.

Even if you have not received all three reports, send a dispute letter to all three CRAs. Know that you are a consumer, so an error on one report could mean the same error is on other reports. It is not a crime disputing with all CRAs. Of course, if you can start the dispute process with one CRA, you will not have much trouble doing with the others. When a CRA cannot find an error, it will respond with a letter informing you about it.

Whether you are using the CRA dispute form or drafting your dispute letter, use only certified mail with the return receipt requested. While a CRA hardly claims not to have received your letter, sending certified mail is still best for your correspondence, especially in cases of pressing legal disputes like identity theft.

Call the CRA to know whether your dispute was received. Note that when talking with CRA agents, be careful not to give them the information you do not want to be included in your report.

The following is a list of CRA customer service phone numbers:

- **Equifax: (800) 685-1111**
- **Experian: (888) 397-3742**
- **TransUnion: (800) 916-8800**

As soon as a CRA gets your dispute letter, it notifies you and then informs you later of the completion of the verification process. You may get a response much sooner than 30 days—it all depends on the number of accounts you are disputing and the speed at which source creditors give back the verification forms. Still, give it up to 40 days. If you do not get anything after 40 days, know that your dispute was not recognized, so send another one.

What Is Found In a CRA's Response to a Dispute?

After receiving your corrected reports, carefully read through them. The first or second page should include a paragraph stating the information reinvestigated upon your request; next is a list of affected accounts and the results of the reinvestigation. Here you will see one or more of the three possible outcomes regarding the dispute process:

1. Deleted: Deleted accounts—like they never existed.

2. Verified—No Change: No changes were made. The accounts will continue to report information

3. Update: This could mean one of three things:

I. Deleted late or past due indications.

II. After the review of the account by the source creditor, a small adjustment was made, and it does not affect your report.

III. Along with the forms, the source creditor returns an updated submission on your file (a requirement after every few months) to update your account. In this case, do not be fooled by the "update" notification, and make sure the first issue has been addressed. If not, send a follow-up letter.

Make Sure Everything Is Readable

No matter what you send, you want to make sure that someone else will be able to read it. This is another reason why having someone proofread your letter is often the best option as they will be able to tell you if something isn't readable or doesn't make sense.

While you should do your best to type as much information as possible, you shouldn't write the letter by hand. While this will be accepted, it is generally not something that people do in this day and age. Furthermore, typing most of the information will ensure that words are not mistaken for another word, which can happen with handwriting. While you might feel your handwriting is easily readable, someone else might not be able to understand it as well.

CHAPTER 14:
609 LETTERS TEMPLATES

It is important to remember that disputing positive items on your credit report is not recommended, even if the information is wrong, because it is difficult to get something placed back onto your record once it is removed. Be sure that you truly want something removed from your credit report and know the effects of doing so before starting this process.

Letter 1: Affidavit of Unknown Inquiries

EQUIFAX

P.O. box 740256

ATLANTA GA 30374

My name Is John William; my current address is 6767. W Phillips Road, Sar Jose, CA 78536, SSN: 454-02-9928, Phone: 415-982-3426, Birthdate: 6-5-1981

I checked my credit reports and noticed some inquiries from companies that I did not give consent to access my credit reports; I am very concerned about all activity going on with my credit reports these days. I immediately demand the removal of these inquiries to avoid any confusion as I DID NOT initiate these inquires or give any form of consent electronically, in person, or over the phone. I am fully aware that without a permissible purpose, no entity is allowed to pull my credit unless otherwise noted in section 604 of the FCRA.

The following companies did not have permission to request my credit report:

CUDL/FIRST CALIFORNIA ON 6-15-2017

CUDL/NASA FEDERAL CREDIT UNION ON 6-15-2017

LOANME INC 3-14-2016

CBNA on 12-22-2017

I once again demand the removal of these unauthorized inquiries immediately.

(Signature)

Thank you

Letter 2: Affidavit of Suspicious Addresses

1-30-2018

ASHLEY WHITE

2221 N ORANGE AVE APT 199

FRESNO CA 93727

PHONE: 559-312-0997

SSN: 555-59-4444

BIRTHDATE: 4-20-1979

EQUIFAX

P.O. box 740256

ATLANTA GA 30374

To whom it may concern:

I recently checked a copy of my credit report and noticed some addresses reporting that do not belong to me or have been obsolete for an extended time. For the safety of my information, I hereby request that the following obsolete addresses be deleted from my credit reports immediately;

4488 N white Ave apt 840 Fresno, CA 93722

4444 W Brown Ave apt 1027 Fresno CA 93722

13330 E Blue Ave Apt 189 Fresno CA 93706

I have provided my identification card and social security card to verify my identity and current address. Please notify any creditors who may be reporting any unauthorized past accounts that are in connection with these mentioned addresses as I have exhausted all of my options with the furnishers.

(Your signature)

This letter is to get a response from the courts to show the credit bureaus that you have evidence that they cannot legally validate the bankruptcy

Letter 3: Affidavit of James Robert

U.S BANKRUPTCY COURT

700 STEWART STREET 6301

SEATTLE, WA 98101

RE: BANKRUPTCY (164444423TWD SEATTLE, WA)

To whom it may concern:

My Name is JAMES ROBERT, my mailing address is 9631 s 2099h CT Kent, WA 99999.

I recently reviewed my credit reports and came upon the above-referenced public record.

The credit agencies have been contacted, and they report in their investigation that you furnished or reported to them that the above matter belongs to me.

This act may have violated federal and Washington state privacy laws by submitting such information directly to the credit agencies, Experian, Equifax, and Transunion via mail, phone, or fax.

I wish to know if your office violated Washington State and federal privacy laws by providing information on the above-referenced matter via phone, fax, or mail to Equifax, Experian, or TransUnion.

Please respond as I have included a self-addressed envelope,

Thank You (your signature)

Letter 4: Affidavit of Erroneous Entry

Dispute letter for bankruptcy to credit bureaus

1-1-18

JAMES LEE

131 S 208TH CT

KENT WA 98031

SSN: 655-88-0000

PHONE: 516-637-5659

BIRTHDATE: 10-29-1985

EXPERIAN

P. O. Box 4500

Allen, TX 75013

RE: BANKRUPTCY (132323993TWD SEATTLE, WA)

To whom it may concern:

My name is James Lee, my mailing address is 131 s 208th CT Kent, WA 98031

I recently disputed the entry of bankruptcy that shows on my credit report, which concluded as a verified entry your bureau. I hereby request your methods of verification; if my request cannot be met, I demand that you delete this entry right away and submit me an updated credit report showing the changes.

Thank you (Your signature)

Letter 5: Affidavit for Account Validation

First letter you send to the credit bureaus for disputes

1-18-2019

TRANSUNION

P.O. BOX 2000

CHESTER PA 19016

To whom it may concern:

My name is John Doe, SSN: 234-76-8989, my current address is 4534. N Folk street Victorville, CA 67378, Phone: 310-672-0929 and I was born on 4-22-1988.

After checking my credit report, I have found a few accounts listed above that I do not recognize. I understand that before any account or information can be furnished to the credit bureaus, all information and all accounts must be 100% accurate, verifiable, and properly validated. I am not disputing the existence of this debt, but I deny that I am the responsible debtor. I am also aware that mistakes happen; I believe these accounts can belong to someone else with a similar name or with my information used without my consent, either from the furnisher itself or an individual.

I am demanding physical documents with my signature or any legally binding instruments that can prove my connection to these erroneous entries. Failure to fully verify that these accounts are accurate is a violation of the FCRA and must be removed, or it will continue to damage my ability to obtain additional credit from this point forward.

I hereby demand that the accounts listed above be legally validated or be removed from my credit report immediately.

Thank you (Your signature)

Letter 6: Affidavit of Request for Method Verification

Second letter to Credit Bureau if they verified anything

10-22-17

JOSHUA ETHAN

2424 E Dawn Hill way

Merced, CA 93245

SSN: 555-22-3333

Phone: 415-222-9090

Birthdate: 9-29-1987

EQUIFAX

P.O. BOX 740256

ATLANTA GA 30374

To whom it may concern:

I recently submitted a request for investigation on the following accounts, which were determined as verified:

Acct Numbers# (XXXXXXX COLLECTION AGENCY A)

(XXXXXXX COLLECTION AGENCY B)

I submitted enough information for you to carry out a reasonable investigation of my dispute; you did not investigate this account or account(s) thoroughly enough as you chose to verify the disputed items.

Under section 611 of the FCRA, I hereby request the methods in which you verified these entries. If you cannot provide me with a reasonable reinvestigation and the methods of which you used for verification, please delete these erroneous entries from my credit report. Furthermore, I would like to be presented with all relevant documents about the disputed entries.

I look forward to resolving this manner

(Your signature)

Letter 7: Affidavit of Method Verification

Second letter to a collection agency if they verified anything

1-30-2018

JAMES DAVID

1111 N FAIR AVE APT 101

FRESNO CA 93706

PHONE: 559-399-0999

SSN: 555-59-5599

BIRTHDATE: 9-25-1979

EXPERIAN

P. O. BOX 4500

ALLEN, TX 75013

To whom it may concern:

I previously disputed this account with your company, and it resulted in you verifying this entry. I am once again demanding validation of this debt for the second time as I have yet to receive sufficient documentation that legally shows I am responsible for this matter.

In addition to requesting validation, I am formally requesting your method of verification for these entries that I have previously disputed. Please supply me with any documentation you may have on file to aid your stance.

If this entry cannot be validated or if the method of verification cannot be provided to me promptly, I demand that you delete this entry immediately.

Thank you.

(Your signature)

Letter 8: Affidavit of Fraudulent Information

Letter to Credit Bureau for identity theft

10-17-17

HELEN JOHNSON

2525 S CHERRY AVE APT 201

FRESNO, CA 93702

PHONE 559-299-2328

BIRTHDAY 11-30-1990

SOCIAL SECURITY NUMBER 555-89-1111

EQUIFAX CONSUMER

FRAUD DIVISION

P.O. BOX 740256

ATLANTA GA 30374

To whom it may concern:

I am writing this letter to document all of the accounts reported by these furnishers that stem from identity theft. I have read and understood every right I have under section 605B and section 609 of the FCRA. Please block the following accounts that are crippling my consumer reports as I do not recognize, nor am I responsible for, nor have I received any money or goods from the creation of these unknown accounts.

Please refer to Police Report and ID Theft Affidavit attached.

1) CBE GROUP (12323239XXXX)

2) LOBEL FINANCIAL (431XXXX)

Please contact each credit to prevent further charges, activity, or authorizations of any sort regarding my personal information.

Thank you (Your signature)

Letter 9: Affidavit of Fraudulent Information

Letter to lender or collection agency when reporting fraudulent accounts

10-15-17

TARA BROWN

3421 N ROSE AVE APT 211

OAKLAND CA 93766

PHONE 559-369-9999

BIRTHDAY 9-20-1979

SOCIAL SECURITY NUMBER 584-00-0222

MONTGOMERY WARD

RE Account # 722222XXXX

TRANSUNION

P.O. BOX 2000

CHESTER PA 19016

To whom it may concern:

I have recently reviewed my credit reports and found an account listed that I do not recognize. I am informing you today that you are reporting the above-mentioned account that is a result of identity theft, and continuing to report this entry will be in violation of FACTA rules and regulations.

I have never had this account MONTGOMERY WARD 99986518XXXX, and I ask that you cease all reporting and collection activity surrounding this account which is my right under section 605B of the FCRA. Please refer to a police report.

I ask that this information be blocked and disregarded by your accounting. Thank you for your time, and I will be eagerly waiting for your response.

Thank you (Your signature)

CONCLUSION

You can repair your credit. It's not a fast fix, but it can start happening this month. Follow the suggestions and guidelines in this book to raise your score from the depths up to a number you're happy to see. You can get your slice of the American dream with your dream house, financial security, and peace of mind. A journey of a thousand miles begins with a single step, and within a year, you can get your credit score up to the point where conventional lenders will start looking at you again. You don't deserve the shame and embarrassment of no one being there for you when your cash is short, and by learning to play the games of the credit card companies and debt collectors, you put yourself back on track to get everything you want in life.

www.ingramcontent.com/pod-product-compliance
Lightning Source LLC
LaVergne TN
LVHW022315200926
848481LV00004B/1359